1926 MANUAL OF DOMESTIC ART (COOKERY)

Editor
Geoffrey Higges

Extracts from the textbook
"Manual of Domestic Art (Cookery)"
a manual of rules and recipes compiled in 1926
by
Miss Ellie Campbell Dip. Dom. Ec.
Inspector of Domestic Arts
in the South Australian Education Department

Edited by Geoffrey Higges

.

CONTENTS

ACKNOWLEDGMENTS

Thank you to my wife Carole-Anne Fooks for
proofreading.
Note: Unusual or dated wording and procedures have not
been changed. Some spelling has been updated.

1 BASIC RULES AND DEFINITIONS

A Recipe

A recipe consists of 3 parts:

(a) The name.

(b) The list of ingredients.

(c) The method.

Before beginning to follow a recipe, it is necessary to read it through carefully, noting the time required for cooking and the method of cooking employed.

Order of Work

1. Attend to the fire or oven.

2. Collect all utensils needed.

3. Collect and prepare all ingredients

4. Work neatly and clear away as you work.

Food

Food is any substance which, when taken into the body, helps to sustain life.

Reasons for Cooking

1. Food is rendered more readily digestible.

2. Flavours are developed, and food is more palatable.

3. Food is preserved by destroying the germs that may be present.

4. The appearance is changed.

Good Cooking

A knowledge of the methods of cooking applied to different foods is necessary, for bad cooking may spoil good food and injure digestion.

 Well cooked meals give pleasure and promote good health.

2 BUYING AND STORING FOOD

Rules for Buying Food

1. Buy from firms which do good business and have a large turnover, so their goods are fresher.
2. Buy good brands of groceries.
3. Buy soap, candles, matches and sugar in large quantities.
4. Buy in small quantities all groceries that:
(a) lose their flavour by exposure, such as tea, coffee and spices,
(b) become musty – flour,
(c) weevils - oatmeal, cayenne.
5. Buy foods that are in season, so cheap and plentiful.
6. Pay cash wherever possible.

Choice of Food

Meat - should be firm to the touch, have a bright colour, the fat firm and yellow in beef, white in mutton and pork; should be moist but not slimy.

Fish - must be perfectly fresh; the signs are:
(1) bright eyes,
(2) firm flesh,
(3) red gills,
(4) fresh smell.

Vegetables - should be crisp, not wilted or withered; have a good colour, and have a pleasant smell,
(a) **root vegetables** have the parts that are eaten grow underground like carrots, parsnips, turnips, onions and beetroots,
(b) **green vegetables** have the parts which are eaten grow above ground, like cabbage, peas, beans, marrow, celery, cauliflower, and spinach.

Eggs - If bought when plentiful, eggs should be preserved for the winter months. Fresh eggs are clear when held up to the light and sink when placed in cold water, bad eggs float.

Dried Fruits - should be bought at the beginning of the season.

Tinned Foods - a supply may be kept in reserve to be used in emergencies. Choose tins that are in good condition and show no signs of bulging.

Storage of Food

Groceries

(1) Groceries should all be kept in jars or tins with well fitted lids, and well labelled. No paper bags or packets should be left on shelves or cupboards as they attract vermin.

(2) Salt and sugar should not be kept in tins.

(3) Flour must be kept off the floor in a dry place.

(4) Soap should be cut up when fresh and kept on a shelf in the laundry.

(5) Keep bottled fruits and jam in a cool, dry place, not exposed to strong light.

Perishable Foods

Meat - should be hung in a fly-proof safe or well-ventilated pantry; or use a bag of cheese cloth kept in shape by hoops or wire or bamboo to hang in a shady place out of doors. Meat may be sprinkled with pepper if it has to be kept a long time.

Dip a cloth in vinegar, wring it out, and wipe the meat well before cooking.

Milk and Butter - should be kept in the coolest place, away from strong smelling foods.

Cheese - should be wrapped in butter paper and covered from the air.

Root Vegetables - may be kept in a clean box or may be put in the ground and lightly covered with soil.

Onions - are best kept in a string bag or hanging in a bunch.

3 FOOD CLASSES

Group 1 - building foods.
Foods, containing proteins, that build the tissues and
muscles of the body, such as milk, meat, fish, cheese, beans
and cereals. Some of the proteins that are enjoyed each day
are albumen, casein, gluten, gelatine and fibrin.
Group 2 - strengthening and purifying foods.
Foods containing mineral salts that build bones and other
tissues such as fruit, vegetables, cereals, milk and eggs. Salts
which are in most foods are soda salt, iron salt, magnesia
salt, potash salt, lime salt, phosphate salt and sulphur salt.
Group 3 - heat giving foods (carbohydrates).
Foods containing the carbohydrates starch and sugar that
supply fuel for production of heat and energy, such as
potatoes, cereals, fruit, honey, treacle and jam.
Group 4 - heat giving foods (fats).
Fuel foods that contain fat such as butter, cream, oil, nuts,
meat, eggs and milk.
Group 5 – liquids.
Water, which is found in all foods, is needed to form the
fluids of the body.
Group 6 – helpers.
(a) Vitamins - substances which are essential to health
found in green vegetables, whole cereals, citrus and other
fruits, eggs, milk and milk products. Vitamins are known by
letters of the alphabet like A, B1, B2, C and D.
(b) Cellulose - roughage which is the indigestible part of
fruits and vegetables.
Milk is the most valuable food:
(1) Skim the cream from the surface of a glass of milk; stir
it in a basin until butter is formed. This is the fat of milk.
The remaining liquid is butter milk, which is slightly sweet.

(2) Add a few drops of lemon juice or vinegar to a cup of milk. The milk separates into curds, containing the protein, and whey, containing water, lime and sugar etc.

(3) Milk gives no blue colour when iodine is added, thus showing the absence of starch.

Foods that can take the place of meat

1. Cheese - consisting of 1/3 protein, 1/3 fat and 1/3 water.

2. Eggs - 15% protein.

3. Dried Peas and Beans - contain the protein legumin; should be cooked for a long time or made into soup.

4 VEGETABLES

General Rules for Cooking Vegetables

Root vegetables should be put into boiling salted water and boiled slowly with the lid on the saucepan - except old potatoes which should be put into cold salted water. (One heaped teaspoonful of salt to every quart of water.)

Green vegetables should be put into boiling salted water and boiled rapidly with the lid off the saucepan - except sugar should be used instead of salt for green peas and broad beans; spinach should be washed thoroughly and cooked in little or no extra water.

All vegetables can be cooked by steam.

When baking vegetables the fat should be very hot before the vegetables are added.

Do not overcook vegetables.

Never allow prepared vegetables to stand in water or fat – strain them as soon as they are cooked.

The water used for cooking vegetables may be used for stock.

Note whether the lid should be kept on or off.

Draining Methods

Old Potatoes - drain against the lid of the saucepan.

Cauliflower and Marrow - drain on lifter and then on toast.

Cabbage and Spinach - drain in colander and press with a saucer.

Peas and Beans - drain in colander, return to the pan, then toss over the fire with butter and pepper to saute.

Root Vegetables - drain in colander or on lifter.

Steamed Vegetables - need very little draining (except cabbage).

Baked Vegetables - drain on crumpled paper.

All vegetables should be served in hot vegetable dishes.

White Vegetable Sauce

Ingredients

1 ounce (28 grams) of butter

Half an ounce of flour

Quarter pint (120 ml) of vegetable liquor

Half a gill (70 ml) of milk

Method - Melt the butter in a small saucepan, then take it off the fire and add the flour. Stir till smooth. Add the milk and vegetable liquor and put back on the fire. Stir till boiling, then cook for 2 minutes. Serve very hot.

How to Cook Potatoes

1. Old Potatoes - scrub to clean, dry with a dishcloth, put in a bowl of clean water, peel thinly, place in the bowl of water for a short time, put the potatoes in a saucepan with just enough water to cover them, bring to the boil, add salt, boil gently until tender (test with skewer).

Strain against the lid of the saucepan, tilting the saucepan 3 times to be sure all the water is drained off, then steam the potatoes by tucking a piece of flannel or tea towel over them, placing the lid on tightly, and steaming for 3 minutes. Lift the potatoes carefully out of the saucepan with a spoon, into a hot vegetable dish. Put a lid on the vegetable dish and serve.

2. New Potatoes - scrub the potatoes, scrape off the skin, place in a bowl of water. Put water on to boil, just sufficient to cover the potatoes, when boiling add salt, the potatoes and a sprig of mint.

Cook gently until the potatoes are tender and strain against the lid of the saucepan. Add half a teaspoonful of butter and 10 shakes of pepper. Shake the saucepan over the fire to melt the butter and drive off any remaining water, i.e. saute. Serve in a hot vegetable dish.

3. Baked Potatoes - choose potatoes of an even size. Wash, peel thinly and dry. Sprinkle with salt. Place under the meat one hour before serving. Turn once to brown on both sides. Drain on paper before serving.

4. Steamed Potatoes - prepare as for boiling, sprinkle with salt and cook in an enamel or aluminium steamer until tender. Lift out on to a hot dish.

5. Mashed Potatoes - break up the cooked potatoes with a fork, add butter and hot milk, beat over the fire until light and creamy.

How to Cook Carrots, Turnips and Cabbage

1. Carrots (and Parsnips) - wash well, scrape the skin off and place in a bowl of water. Put on to boil with just enough water to cover the carrots, and when boiling cut the carrots into serving sizes and add salt. Boil slowly with the lid on until tender. Lift out with a wire lifter, or drain through a colander and place in a hot vegetable dish.

2. Turnips - wash, peel thickly and cut into neat pieces. Bring to the boil just enough water to cover the vegetables then add the turnips and salt. Boil slowly with the lid on till tender, lift out the turnips with a wire lifter or drain through a colander. Serve in a hot vegetable dish.

3. Cabbage - remove the outer broken leaves and the thick end of the stalk. Make a crosscut through the stalk end, going halfway through the cabbage. Soak in a bowl of salted water. Boil sufficient water to cover the cabbage, and when boiling add salt and then the cabbage after draining well. Boil rapidly with the lid off until tender.

Lift out the cabbage with two wire lifters and put in a colander. Press down on the cabbage with a saucer to remove all the water. Place in a hot vegetable dish and cut into neat squares. Sprinkle with pepper and place small pieces of butter along the cuts. Serve very hot. (Do not empty the cabbage water down a sink inside the house on account of the unpleasant odour.)

How to use Toast in Vegetable Cooking

Pumpkin - put the water on to boil and cut the pumpkin into even sized pieces for serving, and peel thinly. When the water is boiling, add salt and the vegetables. Boil with the lid off until tender, then lift the pieces of pumpkin out very carefully with a wire lifter and place on a slice of toast in a hot vegetable dish. Mask with a vegetable sauce and sprinkle lightly with chopped parsley.

Onions and Leeks - put the water on to boil, peel the outer covering off the vegetables and place them in a bowl of water. When the water is boiling, add salt, vegetables and one teaspoonful of sugar.

Boil gently with the lid on until tender, then lift with a wire lifter and place on a slice of toast in the hot vegetable dish. Mask with vegetable sauce.

Cauliflower - cut most of the green leaves off and place the cauliflower in a bowl of salted water to draw off any insects. Put water on to boil, and when boiling put in salt and the cauliflower, with the flower part down. Boil gently with the lid off for 10 minutes, then turn the cauliflower over, stalk down. Skim well while cooking. Lift out the cauliflower with two wire lifters, and place on a slice of toast in a hot vegetable dish. Mask with a vegetable sauce and sprinkle lightly with chopped parsley.

How to Cook Peas and Beans

Peas - shell the peas into a colander and wash them. Put water on to boil, but just before it boils add a sprig of mint, one teaspoonful of sugar, and the peas. Boil very gently with the lid off until the peas are tender. Strain them through a colander then return them to the saucepan and add butter, pepper and salt. Toss over the fire until the butter is melted and moisture is driven off (sauteing) and serve in a hot vegetable dish.

French Beans - put water in a saucepan to boil. String the beans by cutting a very narrow strip on each side, remove a small piece at each end, then wash the beans, and cut them into long, thin slanting pieces. When the water is boiling, add salt and the beans. Boil rapidly with the lid off until the beans are tender, removing the scum as it rises. Strain through a colander, return to the saucepan, add butter and pepper. Saute, then serve in a hot vegetable dish.

Broad Beans - heat just sufficient water to cover the beans, shell them into a colander, and wash them. When the water is hot but not boiling, add salt and the beans. Boil gently with the lid off until tender. Strain through a colander, return to the saucepan, add butter and pepper. Saute, then serve in a hot vegetable dish with sauce if desired.

.

5 SOUP

1. Soup should be the first course in a meal because it aids digestion by producing a flow of gastric juice in the stomach.
2. Soup whets the appetite.
3. Soup supplies water and mineral salts to the body.

Classes of Soup

1. Self-contained Soup - when the nourishment is contained in the ingredients, as in Cottage Broth and Gravy Soup.
2. Stock Soup - when the foundation of the soup is stock, such as Macaroni Soup and Julienne Soup.
3. Puree - when the whole contents of the saucepan are mashed through a sieve, returned to the saucepan, reheated and thickened, as Soup Maigre and Tomato Soup.
Moistened Flour is added to a puree when it is reheated to bring the mashed vegetables and give an even thickness.
Other thickeners used in soups are sago, tapioca, macaroni and barley.

Definitions and Rules Related to Making Soup

Bouquet Garni - 3 sprigs of parsley, 2 sprigs of thyme, 1 sprig of marjoram and 1 bay leaf, tied together - used for flavouring stock, soup and stew.
Croutons - small cubes of fried or toasted bread used as a garnish for soups.
Stock - the liquid obtained by cooking bones, meat, vegetables and herbs for several hours, then straining.
Second Stock - the liquid obtained by cooking bones cooked the day before, with fresh vegetables, for some hours, then straining.

Rules for Making Stock

1. Use a saucepan with a tight lid.
2. Allow 1 pint (1/2 litre) of water for every pound (1/2

kg) of bones, plus 1 pint to allow for evaporation.

3. Cut meat off bones and put both into salted cold water to extract the goodness. Bring slowly to the boil.

4. Remove scum as it rises.

5. Add herbs and cut-up vegetables.

6. Allow to simmer until cooked - this will soften the gelatine and draw out the goodness.

7. Strain through a colander.

8. Remove fat when cold.

Other Rules Related to Making Soup

1. Vegetables for self-contained and stock soups should be cut into very small cubes.

2. Vegetables for purees should be cut up roughly, as they are mashed through a sieve when cooked.

3. Garnish self-contained and stock soups with chopped parsley.

4. Garnish purees with croutons.

5. Remove fat from soup before serving, first with a spoon, then with pieces of kitchen paper.

6. Serve soup in a hot soup tureen.

Selected Recipes for Making Soup

Mutton Broth

Ingredients

2 shanks or 1 pound (1/2 kg) neck mutton

1 carrot, 1 turnip, 1 onion

2 stalks of celery

Pepper, and 2 teaspoonfuls (10 ml) salt

Parsley, and 3 ounces (85 gm) barley

Method - Cut meat, with fat removed, into fine dice. Wash the barley, then put meat, bones, barley, salt, pepper and water into saucepan and bring slowly to the boil. Wash and peel the vegetables, cut into very fine dice, then add to the soup when it is boiling. Simmer for up to 3 hours. Remove any fat and season to taste. Garnish with very finely chopped parsley and serve very hot.

Soup Maigre

Ingredients

1 1/2 pounds (680 gm) potatoes

1 parsnip, 1 onion, 1 turnip

2 white onions or leeks, 2 sticks celery

1 teaspoon (5 ml) sugar, 2 teaspoon (10 ml) salt

1 desert spoon (30 gm) fat

2 quarts (1.9 litres) water

1 1/2 ounces (40 gm) flour

1 pint (480 ml) milk

Method - Wash and peel all vegetables and cut them up roughly.

Make fat hot in a saucepan then add vegetables, salt and sugar. Stir for 3 minutes, not allowing to brown. Add the water, bring to the boil, allow to simmer until the vegetables are tender. Rub the contents of the pan through a sieve or colander to make puree. Return to the saucepan and re-heat. Add the milk, then when boiling add a little water blended with the flour. Remove fat and season to taste.

Season with croutons and serve hot.

Tomato Soup

Ingredients

2 pounds (900 gm) tomatoes

1 large onion

1 tablespoon (14 gm) dripping

1 teaspoon (5 ml) salt, 1 teaspoon sugar

3 pints (1.4 litres) water, 1 pint (480 ml) milk

Quarter teaspoon (3.5 ml) carbonate of soda

1 tablespoon (14 gm) cornflour

Method - Wash tomatoes and peel onions, and cut them up roughly, then fry in hot dripping in a saucepan. Add salt and sugar, then add water and bring to the boil. Simmer until the vegetables are tender.

Mash through a sieve then return to the saucepan and bring to the boil again. Add carbonate of soda, milk and moistened cornflour.

When the cornflour is cooked, remove the fat and season to taste.

Garnish with croutons and serve hot.

6 MEAT

Properties of Meat

1. Meat is rich in proteins and fats but is deficient in carbohydrates.
2. It is a muscle building food, furnishes heat and energy, and is stimulating and satisfying.
3. Excessive meat eating is harmful, and other muscle building foods such as eggs, cheese, fish and milk should replace it to a certain extent. This is especially so in hot seasons.
4. Beef is more nutritious than mutton.
5. Pork is indigestible because of its richness in fat.
6. Veal and lamb are less nutritious; being the flesh of young animals they have a larger proportion of water.
7. Meat that has little or no fat has very poor flavour.
8. All meat must be cooked slowly to be tender.

Assessing the Quality of Meat

1. Meat should have a healthy red colour.
2. The lean should be firm to the touch and elastic.
3. The fat should be firm and dry.
4. Meat should not make the fingers wet or clammy.
5. The flesh should have a marbled appearance.
6. The odour should not be noticeable.
7. The lean should contain plenty of red juices.
8. Meat should not shrink much when cooked; roasting will cause more shrinkage than boiling.
9. Salted meat should have a clean, velvety feeling.

The Structure of Meat

Meat consists of numbers of fibres bound together in bundles. These fibres are hollow tubes containing the red juices. If the meat is cut across the fibres the juices escape, and the meat loses flavour. To retain the juices the pores of the muscle tubes should be sealed off by the application of heat.

Methods of Cooking Meat

1. Baking - cooking by hot air in an enclosed oven. It is the most usual way of cooking meat, poultry, pies and cakes.

2. Grilling or Broiling - cooking by exposure to direct heat from either a red fire or the heated bars of a gas stove. It is suitable for small pieces of meat, fish, chops and steak.

3. Boiling - cooking by covering with boiling water at 212 degrees Fahrenheit or 100 degrees Celsius. This temperature is maintained for vegetables and puddings, but for meat is reduced to simmering (175 degrees Fahrenheit or 80 degrees Celsius).

4. Steaming - cooking in the steam from boiling water. It is a longer process than boiling, and is suitable for light puddings and vegetables, or for less tender cuts of meat.

5. Stewing - the slow cooking of meat and vegetables in a small quantity of liquid at 180 degrees Fahrenheit or less. This is the most economical method of cooking, as the juices and flavour extracted form part of the stew. Also cheaper cuts of meat may be used, and not so much heat is required in the cooking.

In making brown stews (from red meats) the meat is generally fried in the saucepan first; in white stews (white meats) milk is usually added. White stews can be easily digested while still nourishing, and so are suitable for invalids.

6. Frying - Cooking in hot fat or oil at a temperature of 360 degrees Fahrenheit or 185 degrees Celsius. Although the quickest way of cooking, it is the least suitable for meat, the high temperatures being apt to harden the fibres making it indigestible. Deep frying (French) is suitable for foods that take a short time to cook, such as fritters, rissoles and fish fillets. Shallow frying (English) is suitable for foods that take longer to cook, such as cutlets, lamb's fry and sausages.

7. Braising - the meat is stewed and baked simultaneously in a braising pan.

Preferred Cooking Method for Different Cuts of Meat
Beef
1. Baking - sirloin, ribs, topside.
2. Boiling (corned) - silverside, aitch bone, brisket.
3. Stewing - chuck steak, skirt steak, shin.
4. Grilling - fillet and rump steaks.
5. Soup - shin, leg.

Mutton
1. Baking - leg, loin, shoulder, saddle.
2. Boiling - leg, neck, head.
3. Stewing - neck, breast.

Selected Recipes Using Meat
Baked Beef, Mutton or Lamb

Method - Weigh the joint and calculate the time to cook - for red meats 15 minutes per pound or half kilogram, plus 15 minutes (for white meat read 20 minutes). Prepare the oven and light the fire so that it is very hot before putting in the meat. Wipe the joint with a damp cloth. Roll beef and skewer it. Remove the outer skin from mutton or lamb (not the fat) and tie into a nice shape if necessary.

Do not sprinkle salt or flour on the meat before cooking. Put 3 good tablespoons of dripping in a baking dish and place the meat on a stand in the dish.

Put the dish in the hottest part of the oven. After 10 minutes decrease the heat. Baste the meat every 15 minutes. When the meat is cooked place it on to a hot meat dish. Pour nearly all the fat out of the baking dish, leaving about one tablespoonful. Add one desertspoon of flour (or less for thin gravy for red meats), half a teaspoon of salt and a little pepper. Fry until it is a nice rich brown; stir well. Add half a pint (1/4 litre) of stock or water and stir till boiling; boil for 3 minutes. Strain into a gravy boat. Serve the meat and gravy hot.

Note - Vegetables or Yorkshire pudding may be baked in the dish under the meat.

Boiled Mutton and Suet Dumplings

Ingredients

3 pounds (1 1/3 kg) best end neck mutton

Root vegetables - 2 carrots, 2 turnips, 2 onions

Water, parsley sauce, suet dumplings (see under)

Method - Weigh the meat and allow 20 minutes for every pound or half kilogram, plus an additional 20 minutes. Wipe meat well with a cloth wrung out in hot water. Put the meat in a saucepan of boiling water, placing the part downwards that will be served upwards. Boil for 5 minutes, then simmer for the rest of the time. One hour before serving time, scrape or peel the root vegetables and put them in the saucepan of simmering water. having made the dumplings as under, put them in the same saucepan and cook for half an hour. Make parsley sauce. When cooked, lift the meat on to a hot dish and place the dumplings around. Serve the vegetables in a vegetable dish, and sauce in a sauce bowl.

Suet Dumplings

Method - Sift half a pound (225 grams) of flour with half a teaspoon of baking powder. Shred a 1/4 pound (110 grams) of suet and rub it into the flour. Add one desertspoon of chopped parsley and a pinch of salt. Mix with a 1/4 pint (120 ml) of water into a stiff crust. Cut into 6 pieces, roll into balls, and cook in boiling water for half an hour.

Irish Stew
Ingredients
1 pound (450 grams) of best end neck of mutton, or neck
chops, 2 pounds (900 grams) of potatoes, 2 onions
3/4 pint (350 ml) water, pepper and salt
Method - Skin and trim the chops but leave most of the fat
on. Cut the meat into sizes convenient for serving and put
into a saucepan; sprinkle with pepper and salt; add the
water and bring slowly to the boil. Add the onions cut into
rings, and simmer gently for one hour.
Add the potatoes; sprinkle on more pepper and salt, and
simmer for another half an hour, or until the potatoes are
tender. Serve on a hot dish, with meat in the centre, the
onions on top, and the potatoes around the meat.

Grilled Steak or Chops
Ingredients
1 pound (1/2 kg) rump steak, or loin chops
Butter/green butter, pepper and salt, chopped parsley
Method - The steak/chops should be 1 inch (25 mm)
thick. Have a clear, bright fire, or if using a gas stove, light
the griller and let it get hot. Grease the bars of the grill and
make hot. Cut the steak into convenient pieces and put the
meat on the grid. Turn with a knife or spoon every 3
minutes. Cook for 10 to 14 minutes depending as required
and dish quickly on to a hot plate. Rub on a little butter,
sprinkle with pepper and salt, cover with another hot plate
and serve.

Shepherd's Pie
Ingredients
1/2 pound (225 kg) cold cooked meat
1 pound (1/2 kg) mashed potatoes
1/4 teaspoon mixed herbs, 1 very small onion
1/4 pint (120 ml) stock or water
1 teaspoon dripping, 1 teaspoon flour, pepper and salt

Method - Cook the potatoes. Remove fat from the meat and mince it, mixing in the herbs, pepper and salt. Melt dripping in a saucepan and brown the onion nicely. Add flour and brown. Add stock or water, stir while it boils for 3 minutes. Allow to cool slightly then add the meat. Line a greased piedish with potatoes, put in the mixture and spread potatoes on top. Dot with butter and brown lightly. Garnish with parsley and serve hot.

7 FISH

Properties of Fish and How to Choose Fish
Fish is the lightest form of solid food and is suitable for invalids, the aged and growing children.

Fish meat consists of albumen, gelatine, oil, phosphorus, lime and water.

Tinned, dried or smoked fish forms a good substitute for meat and may be made up into many appetising dishes.

Classes of Fish
1. White Fish, where the oil is contained in the liver only, such as whiting, bream and garfish.

2. Oily Fish, where the oil is distributed throughout the flesh, like salmon, eel and herring. Oily fish are more nutritious than white fish, but not so easily digested.

3. Shellfish, such as crayfish, crabs, oysters and mussels are not really fish.

How to Choose Fish
1. The eyes should be bright and prominent.
2. The flesh should be firm to touch.
3. The gills should be bright red.
4. The scales should not come off easily.
5. The smell should be good.
6. Shellfish should be difficult to open.
7. The tail of a lobster should spring back sharply after stretching out.

Methods of Cooking and How to Scale and Fillet Fish
1. Boiling - suitable for large fish with white flesh, and coarser fleshed fish, such as schnapper, bream and cod.

2. Frying - all varieties of small fish such as whiting, mullet and garfish, and larger fillets.

3. Steaming - for small delicate fish like whiting and garfish.

4. Baking - for dry fish like flathead.

5. Grilling - for small fish, and fillets of larger fish.

6. Stewing - needed for large coarse fish.

Cold fish may be made into patties or rissoles.

Bones and heads may be used for fish stock or soups.

How to Scale a Fish

1. Work over a large clean sheet of paper.

2. Scale with back of knife, from tail upwards; be sure to remove every scale.

3. Wash under running water, then wipe with a clean cloth.

How to Fillet Fish

1. Place the scaled fish flat on a fish board, leaving the head and tail on.

2. With a sharp knife: cut the skin up the centre of the back, round under the fins near the head, down the centre of the front and across the tail. Do the same on the other side of the fish.

3. Loosen the skin at the back near the head, hold the fish firmly on the board and draw the skin off from head to tail. Do the same on the other side of the fish. Be careful not to break the flesh.

4. Place a sharp knife between the flesh and the backbone; hold the fish firmly and carefully draw the knife down, separating the flesh from the backbone. Do the same on the other side of the fish.

5. Carefully draw out any bones that may be left in the pieces of flesh.

6. Wash the fillets and dry well.

Notes

1. Fillets may be fried, steamed or grilled.

2. Fillet fish for invalids and small children.

3. The odour of fish may be removed by a cloth boiled in soda.

4. The board used for fish should not be used for meat or pastry until it has been well scrubbed.

Selected Recipes Using Fish
Fried Fillet of Fish
Ingredients
3 large white fish - e.g. whiting, mullet or pike
Breadcrumbs, frying fat
One teaspoon of flour, one teaspoon of salt, pepper
1 egg, or 1 gill (140 ml) of milk
Lemon and parsley to garnish
Method - Clean and fillet fish. Wash in cold salted water
and dry on a clean towel. Mix flour, pepper and salt
together on a plate, and beat up the egg on another plate.
Put breadcrumbs on a piece of kitchen paper. Dip each
fillet first into the flour mixture, then into the egg, and then
toss into the breadcrumbs. Lift out of the breadcrumbs
with a skewer, then firm the crumbs onto the fish with a
knife. Drop the fillets into a saucepan containing hot fat,
and fry about 3 minutes until golden brown. Lift out, drain
on paper, and arrange on a hot dish.
Garnish with slices of lemon and small tips of parsley
which have been fried and drained.
Steamed Fish
Ingredients
Filleted fish
A squeeze of lemon juice
A little milk, pepper and salt
Method - Roll each fillet, white side out, and place on a
deep enamel plate. Sprinkle with salt, pepper and lemon
juice. Put a little milk in the plate. Place the plate over
boiling water and cook for 10 minutes, or until the fish is
white and tender. Serve hot with sauce.
Smoked Fish
Ingredients
Fish, eg blue cod, shetland or barracoota
Pepper, 1 ounce (30 grams) of butter

Method - Put the fish into a saucepan of boiling water. Draw the saucepan off the fire and allow to stand for 15 minutes. Lift out the fish and grill over a clear fire for about 3 minutes on each side, then lift out on to a hot dish. Spread butter over the fish and sprinkle with pepper or serve with a parsley sauce.

Boiled Fish

Ingredients

Bream or Schnapper

One tablespoon of vinegar

Parsley

One tablespoon salt to 4 quarts (4 litres) of water

White of one egg

Method - Trim the fish, leaving the eyes in. Wash and dry. Boil the water in a flat saucepan or fish kettle, and add salt, vinegar and parsley. Put the fish in and immediately draw the saucepan off the fire. Allow the fish to cook in the hot water until tender, 10 to 20 minutes according to the thickness of the fish. Lift the fish out with a fish slice and put on a doyley on a hot dish. Place the stiff beaten egg in little heaps on slices of lemon around the fish, and sprinkle chopped parsley on top. Serve with parsley, egg or oyster sauce served separately in a sauce boat.

8 PUDDINGS

Puddings supply sugar and starch to the body.

Classes of Pudding

1. Boiled - tied up in a cloth and cooked in boiling water, such as apple pudding and currant pudding.

2. Steamed - put into a mould and cooked by steam, as urney, college and devon pudding.

3. Baked - cooked in the oven, as milk puddings and custards.

Boiled Puddings

Boiled puddings are light, wholesome and nourishing, and are suitable for cold weather. Suet is used as fat. Beef suet is the richer and is generally used; mutton suet is lighter. Suet should be firm and dry, skinned and finely shredded. Boiled puddings should be mixed stiffly so that the flour absorbs the melted fat while cooking, preventing the pudding from becoming sodden. The filling may be meat (eg steak and kidney pudding), fruit (currant, sultana or date pudding) or jam (jam roly).

Boiled puddings should be tied tightly in a floured cloth, leaving room for swelling. The pudding cloth should be free from holes and string tied in a bow ready for ease of undoing. The pudding must be well covered by boiling water the whole time it is cooking. Keep a kettle of boiling water ready for continual replenishment.

Before serving, lift the pudding out of the water, drain for a few minutes, untie the string, and the pudding should turn out of the cloth without sticking.

Steamed Puddings

Steamed puddings are the lightest. They are cooked in a greased basin or mould, with a piece of greased paper over the top. The basin should be only three parts filled to allow the pudding to rise.

There are two ways of steaming puddings:

1. Placing the mould in a covered steamer which is fitted over a saucepan of boiling water.

2. Placing the mould directly in a saucepan of boiling water, making sure the boiling water comes only halfway up the mould.

In both cases the water should be kept boiling to ensure a good supply of steam, but make sure the saucepan does not boil dry.

The fat should be clarified fat or butter (suet takes too long to cook).

Baked Puddings

Milk puddings are nourishing and easily digested. They are made from cereal, milk, eggs and sugar. They are good summer puddings,

and are suitable for children, the aged and invalids.

Rules for Making Milk Puddings or Custards

1. For every 3 ounces (90 grams) of grain allow 1 pint (500 ml) of milk, 1 ounce (30 grams) of sugar, 2 eggs and flavouring.

2. See that the cereal is well cooked.

3. Allow the cereal and milk to cool before the egg is added.

4. Place the piedish containing the custard into a baking dish, with a little water. This will prevent the custard from boiling and curdling.

5. Milk puddings require a moderate oven.

6. To test whether the custard is cooked, shake the piedish a little to see if the custard is set.

7. When serving a custard, stand the piedish on a meat dish, and put a piedish frill or a folded serviette around it.

8. If milk pudding is made without egg, stewed fruit may be served with it - as baked rice or creamed sago.

Selected Recipes for Making Puddings
Steak and Kidney Pudding
Ingredients
1 pound (450 grams) of steak
2 sheep's kidneys
1 gill (140 ml) water
Half teaspoon of salt, quarter teaspoon pepper
1 teaspoon of chopped parsley (if liked)
6 ounces (170 grams) of suet crust
Method - Put a saucepan of water on to boil. Have a greased basin, pudding cloth and piece of string ready. Wipe the meat with a damp cloth and cut into pieces. Remove skin from the kidneys, wash and cut into small pieces. Mix together the meat, kidney, flour, pepper, salt and parsley. Make the suet crust and cut off one third for the top of the basin. Roll out the remainder and line the basin smoothly. Fill with the mixture, add a little water, and wet the edges. Roll out the small piece of pastry and cover the meat, pressing the edges and drawing the crust away from the basin. Tie a pudding cloth over the top, and boil for 2 to 2 1/2 hours. Serve in the basin with a serviette pinned round it.

Marmalade Pudding
Ingredients
3 tablespoons of marmalade, 2 tablespoons of flour
3 cups of breadcrumbs, 1 cup of sugar
1 cup of finely chopped suet, 2 eggs
1 teaspoon of baking powder
Juice of 2 oranges, rind of 1 orange
Method - Mix together flour, suet, breadcrumbs, sugar and baking powder. make a hole in the middle and put in the marmalade, orange juice and rind, and well beaten eggs. Mix all ingredients well together and put into a prepared

pudding cloth. Boil for 2 hours and serve with a sweet sauce or custard.

Steamed Date Pudding

Ingredients

6 ounces (170 grams) flour

1 1/2 ounces (40 grams) butter, 1 1/2 ounces fat

1 egg, half a gill (70 ml) milk

Half a teaspoon baking powder

4 ounces (110 grams) dates, 4 ounces sugar

A pinch of salt

Method - Put a saucepan of water on to boil. Sift the flour, baking powder and salt. Cream the butter, fat and sugar. Add the egg and beat well. Then add the milk, flour and dates, and blend lightly. Put into a greased basin and cover with greased paper. Steam for one and a half hours. Remove the paper, turn on to a warm dish, and serve with sauce.

Rice Pudding

Ingredients

2 or 3 ounces (60 - 80 grams) of rice

1 ounce (30 gram) of sugar

2 eggs, 1 pint (470 ml) of milk, half a pint of water

A pinch of salt, nutmeg

Method - Wash the rice and put into a saucepan containing the water. Cook until soft. Add milk. Beat the eggs and sugar. Turn the rice and milk into a greased piedish and add the beaten egg and sugar. Blend well and grate a little nutmeg on top. Add a few small pieces of butter if at hand. Stand the piedish in a tin of water (to prevent curdling) and bake in an oven until set.

9 CAKES

Methods and Rules of Cake Making
3 Methods of Cake Making

1. Beat butter and sugar to a cream; add the moist ingredients and then the dry ingredients (as in plain cake and fruit cake).
2. Beat eggs and sugar until stiff, then fold in flour (as in sponge cakes).
3. Rub butter into flour; add other dry ingredients and then the moist ingredients (scones, rock cakes).

Rules for Cake Making

1. Attend to the oven.
2. Prepare cake tins, or oven slides. Large cake tins are lined with folded greased paper which should be 2 inches (5 cm) higher than the tin. Just grease the tin for sponges or for small patty cakes.
3. Prepare the fruit. It is best cleaned with flour. See that the fruit is quite dry or the cake will become sodden.
4. Always cream butter and sugar thoroughly and beat eggs well.
5. Rich cakes should be mixed more stiffly than plain cakes.
6. When making a fruit cake, fruit and flour should be added alternately.
7. Scones must be quickly mixed, handled as little as possible, and put into the oven at once. Try to get them into the oven within 2 minutes after the milk is added.
8. Always have a decreasing heat. Large cakes should be put into a hot oven and the heat gradually reduced. Plain cakes are put into a moderate oven, and the heat gradually reduced. Small cakes and biscuits are put into a quick oven. Sponges are put into a moderate oven.
9. Never open the oven door until the cake has been in 5 minutes for small cakes or 15 minutes for large cakes.

10. Never close the oven door quickly - this will cause a draught of cold air which might spoil the cake.

11. To test whether the cake is cooked - for sponge and little cakes, press the top lightly with the finger and it will be elastic if cooked; for fruit and plain cakes, a skewer run through the thickest part of the cake should come out dry.

12. Do not test the cake too frequently.

13. Remove the cake from the tin as soon as it is taken from the oven.

14. Likewise remove any paper from the cake immediately, and place the cake on a wire stand, or on a well folded tea towel, to cool.

15. Do not allow the cake to stand in a draught to cool.

16. Do not store fresh cake in the same container as stale cake.

17. Never ice or decorate or cut a cake until it is completely cold.

18. Rich cakes will keep a little longer if a little spirit has been added.

Selected Cake Recipes

Rock Buns

Ingredients

6 ounces (170 grams) flour

2 to 3 ounces of dripping

2 ounces of sugar, 2 ounces of currants or sultanas

Quarter teaspoon of ground ginger

1 egg, 2 tablespoons of milk

Quarter teaspoon of salt, a little nutmeg

Method - See to the oven. Clean the currants, sift the flour, baking powder and salt. Rub the dripping into the flour. Add the fruit sugar and spices. Mix to a stiff dough with the beaten egg and milk. Put in small rough heaps on a greased oven slide. Bake for 10 minutes in a quick oven.

Christmas Cake
Ingredients
Half a pound (225 grams) of butter
Half a pound of brown sugar, half a pound sultanas
Half a pound of currants, half a pound of raisins
Quarter pound of citron peel, 6 eggs
1 tablespoon of treacle, 1 teaspoon of caramel
1 gill (140 ml) brandy or sherry (if liked)
10 ounces (280 grams) of flour
2 ounces (60 grams) almonds, 2 ounces chopped dates or figs
2 ounces of rice flour
1 teaspoon of mixed spice, 1 teaspoon of baking powder
Method - Attend to the oven. Line the tin with folded paper. Beat the butter and sugar to cream. Add the eggs one at a time and beat well.
Add the sifted flour, and finally the brandy, mixing well. Pour into the prepared tin. Bake in a hot oven for the first 10 minutes, then gradually decrease the heat over a period of about 3 hours. When cooked (skewer test), remove from the oven, remove the cake from the tin and the paper, and place on a cake cooler.

Butter Sponge
Ingredients
4 ounces (115 grams) of flour
2 ounces of sugar, 2 ounces of butter
1 tablespoon of milk
Half a teaspoon of cream tartar
Quarter teaspoon of carbonate of soda
1 egg, pinch of salt
Method - Sift flour, cream of tartar and soda. Beat the butter and sugar to a cream, add the egg, then add milk and flour. Mix and pour into prepared sandwich tins. Bake in a moderate oven for 20 to 30 minutes.

Scones

Ingredients

Half a pound (225 grams) of flour (if self-raising omit next 2 items)

1 heaped teaspoon of cream of tartar

Half a teaspoon of carbonate of soda

1 ounce of butter, 1 1/2 gills (210 ml) of milk

1 teaspoon of sugar (if liked)

Method - Sift the flour, cream of tartar, and soda. Rub in the butter and add the sugar. Pour in the milk at once and stir a little until all the dry flour is absorbed. Turn quickly on to a floured board and knead lightly. Pat out half an inch (13 mm) thick, cut as desired, and brush over with milk. Place on a warm oven sheet and bake quickly (7 to 10 minutes).

10 PASTRY

3 Kinds of Pastry

1. Short Crust - so called because it is crumbly when cooked.

2. Flaky Pastry - so called because it is flaky or in layers when cooked.

3. Suet Crust - made with suet as shortening; used for puddings and dumplings.

Ingredients for Pastry

Half a pound (225 grams) of flour

1 gill (140 ml) of water

Quarter pound of fat or suet

Half teaspoon of baking powder

Pinch of salt

Rules for Making Pastry

1. Pastry should be made in a cool, dry place, put on a clean cold oven slide, and cooked in a hot oven.

2. Sift flour, salt and baking powder to remove lumps, mix thoroughly, and enclose air.

3. Rub fat into the flour with the tips of the fingers, raising the fingers out of the flour so that air may mix with the flour as it falls.

4. Handle pastry as little as possible - lightly and quickly.

5. Do not knead Short or Suet Crust; use as little water as possible; the dough must be stiff and in one lump.

6. Make dough for Puff Pastry fairly moist but knead it well before adding the fat.

7. Sprinkle the board and rolling pin with just enough flour to stop the dough from sticking.

8. Roll the pastry with a firm, steady pressure, away from you – never sideways.

9. Do not roll the pastry too large for the dish.

10. When cutting pastry, make a clean, decisive cut, leaving

no ragged edges.

11. Pastry should not be put over the contents of a pie while they are hot, as the steam will make the underside of the pastry sodden.

12. Glaze meat pies with the yolk of egg or milk to give a brown colour when cooked; glaze fruit pies with either the white of egg and sugar, or sugar and water, to give a very light brown colour when cooked.

13. While cooking, never open the oven door within the first 5 minutes, and as little as possible afterwards.

14. Small holes should be made in the covering of a meat pie to allow gases to escape. Pastry that is to be cooked in an open tart tin should be well pricked with a fork to prevent it from rising too much in the centre.

Selected Recipes Using Pastry

Short Crust

Ingredients

Half a pound (225 grams) of plain flour

A little extra flour for the board

Quarter of a pound of clarified fat

Half a teaspoon of baking powder

1 gill (140 ml) of water, a pinch of salt

Method - Sieve the flour, baking powder and salt. Rub the fat into the flour with the tips of the fingers. Mix into a stiff dough with the water. Place on a lightly floured board and roll into the shape required.

Fruit Pie

Ingredients

2 pounds (910 grams) of fruit, such as plums, apricots, pears or peaches, or rhubarb

A little water if the fruit is not juicy enough

2 ounces (60 grams) of sugar

Half a pound (225 grams) of short crust

Method - Wash the fruit and cut it into moderate size pieces (e.g. half apricot size). Place the fruit, sugar and water in a piedish. Make the short crust and roll it about 1 inch (2 1/2 cm) larger all round than the piedish. Cut off the extra 1 inch strip. Moisten the edge of the piedish with water, and add the cut strip around the edge with the cut edge on the outer. Brush this strip with water and place any remaining pastry on top. Decorate the edge with a fork. Glaze the top with water and sugar. Bake in a hot oven for about half an hour or until cooked. Serve the pie on a meat dish with a pie collar or serviette wrapped around it. The top may be sprinkled with sugar.

Flaky Pastry

Ingredients

Half a pound (225 grams) of plain flour

Half a teaspoon of baking powder

Quarter of a pound of fat

Quarter of a pint of water

A pinch of salt

Method - Have the fat quite free from lumps and well mashed, then divide it into 3 equal parts. Sieve flour, salt and baking powder, then mix into a soft dough with the water. Lift the dough on to a floured board and knead until it is smooth and elastic. Roll it into an oblong 3 times as long as it is wide. Spread small pieces of one third of the fat on to the rolled dough, leaving 1/2 inch (12 mm) margin all round.

Sprinkle with flour and fold into 3, turning the top down first. Turn the pastry round so that the closed side is to the left and roll out again into a 3 x 1 oblong. Put on another third of the fat similarly, and sprinkle, fold, turn and roll again. Repeat the whole process with the final third of fat. Finally sprinkle, fold, turn once more and this time roll out into the shape required. Do not decorate the edge, because a clean cut rises much better. (In a single layer of pastry there should be 12 flakes when baked.)

Apple Pie

Ingredients

2 pounds (900 grams) of apples

8 cloves, 2 teaspoons sugar

1/8 pint (60 ml) water (if the fruit is not very juicy)

1/2 pound (225 grams) of flaky pastry

Method - Wipe and peel the apples, cut them into eighths and core them. Put the apples, cloves, sugar and water into a piedish. Make the flaky pastry and roll it out 1 inch (2.5 cm) larger all round than the piedish. Brush round the piedish with water. Cut off the extra 1 inch strip and add it around the edge with the cut edge on the outer.

Moisten this strip of pastry with water and put the cover on the pie.

Trim the edges, but do not decorate them. Glaze with water and sugar, or with the white of an egg. Bake in a hot oven about 30 to 40 minutes. Serve on a hot plate and place a pie collar round the piedish. Sprinkle the top with sugar. May be served with boiled custard.

11 COOKING FOR INVALIDS

Classes of Diets, and Rules of Cooking
1. Ordinary (Full, or Mixed) Diet consists of meat, bread, vegetables and all fruits.

2. Low Diet consists of liquids, as milk tea, light broths, barley water and thin gruel.

3. Milk Diet consists of milk tea, milk and egg flip, arrowroot, sago custards, and all other dishes made with milk or eggs.

4. Light Diet consists of all vegetables and fruits, with egg, cheese, fish and fowl occasionally. Meat is never included in this diet.

5. Meat Diet consists of all kinds of meat, eggs, cheese, milk, broths and soups.

Rules of Cooking for Invalids
1. Foods for invalids should be nourishing and easily digested: it should be presented daintily.
2. Make the food as tempting as possible.
3. Never serve the same preparation twice.
4. Serve a little at a time, at frequent intervals.
5. Never ask the patient what they would like - bring the food in as a surprise.
6. Never leave food in the sick room.
7. Change the food and garnishing as much as possible.
8. Do not over-flavour the food.
9. Be punctual with meals - never keep the patient waiting for food or a drink.
10. All utensils and dishes should be perfectly clean.
11. Never expose the food to dust or flies.
12. Never serve fatty foods to an invalid.
13. Be careful to follow the doctor's orders.
14. Barley water quenches the thirst and contains minerals.

15. Toast water quenches the thirst and cleanses the mouth and tongue.

16. Gruel is best made from plain oatmeal, but make sure to remove the husks.

17. Milk and eggs form a valuable part of an invalid's diet.

18. Eggs are very nutritious; they can be given raw with orange juice or milk.

19. To give variety, milk may be given with soda or barley water, or with a cereal in the form of gruel, or made into jelly or custard.

20. Fish and poultry are tender, digestible and nourishing.

21. Green vegetables should always be part of an invalid's diet, as they contain vitamins. The best vegetables are spinach, cauliflower and marrow.

22. Fruit should be chosen with great care - it must be quite ripe.

Fruit drinks are beneficial to quench thirst. The pulp of baked apples is useful as a mild laxative.

23. Broths and beef tea are useful as stimulants but have little or no food value - they have no vitamins. There are 3 kinds of beef tea:

(a) Standard, or Slow.

(b) Quickly Made.

(c) Raw (always served in coloured glasses).

Rules for Making Beef Tea

(a) Remove as much fat as possible.

(b) Allow 1 pint (470 ml) of water for 1 pound (450 grams) of meat.

(c) Shred steak finely across the grain, soak in water, add lemon juice and salt to help extract the red juices.

(d) Put in a saucepan and heat slowly, stirring continuously until it changes colour.

(e) Beef tea boiled is beef tea spoiled.

Selected Recipes Suitable for Invalids
Gruel
Ingredients

1 tablespoon of oatmeal

3 gills (430 ml) milk or water

1 teaspoon of sugar

A pinch of salt, grated nutmeg.

Method - Blend the oatmeal with 2 tablespoons of the oatmeal. Heat the remainder of the milk with the salt, then pour it slowly on the oatmeal, stirring all the time. Allow it to stand for 1 minute while the oatmeal settles. Strain the milk into a saucepan, heat and stir until boiling, and then simmer for 10 minutes. Add the sugar and a little grated nutmeg.

Barley Water
Ingredients

1 ounce (28 grams) of pearl barley

1 pint (474 ml) of boiling water

Half a gill (70 ml) of cold water

1 slice of lemon, the juice of 1 lemon

Method - Wash the barley and put it in a saucepan with the cold water. Boil and strain. Put the barley in the boiling water with lemon and sugar to taste. Boil slowly for one hour until reduced to half the quantity. Strain, then add sugar and lemon to taste.

Toast Water
Ingredients

1 thin slice of stale bread

Half a pint (240 ml) of water

A squeeze of lemon

Method - Dry the bread thoroughly in the oven, then toast it until dark brown on both sides. Place in the water, and allow to stand for 1 hour, or until the water is the colour of sherry. Strain through muslin.

Add lemon juice if desired.
Invalid Broth
Ingredients
1 pound (450 grams) of beef steak
Half a pound (220 grams) of best end of neck of veal
Half a pound (220 grams) of best end of neck of mutton
1 small onion, 6 peppercorns, salt
1 tablespoon of rice or barley
1 desertspoon of finely chopped barley
Method - Cut the meat into small pieces and remove the
fat. Put the meat and bones in cold water. Add half a
teaspoon of salt and bring very slowly to the boil. Skim
well, add the peppercorns and cut up onion. Simmer gently
for 2 hours. Strain off into a shallow basin and leave until
cold. Remove the fat, add well-washed rice or barley, and
heat gently for half an hour. Remove all traces of fat with
kitchen paper. Add parsley and serve.

www.ingramcontent.com/pod-product-compliance
Lightning Source LLC
Chambersburg PA
CBHW021147020426
42331CB00005B/934